I0017388

Mastering SAP Transportation Management (TM): A Guide

Table of Contents

Chapter 1: Introduction to SAP Transportation Management

In this chapter, we will provide you with an introduction to SAP Transportation Management (TM) and its role in supply chain management. We'll cover the basic features and capabilities of SAP TM and explore the benefits of implementing this powerful solution.

Section 1: Understanding the Role of SAP Transportation Management

Welcome to the world of SAP Transportation Management (TM)! In this section, we'll help you understand the significance of SAP TM in the broader context of supply chain management.

1.1 What is SAP TM?

SAP TM is a comprehensive solution that enables organizations to efficiently plan, execute, and monitor their transportation processes. It helps businesses streamline their logistics operations, optimize transportation costs, and improve customer service.

1.2 Key Features and Capabilities

SAP TM offers a wide range of features and capabilities to support transportation management activities. Let's explore some of the key functionalities:

Order management: SAP TM allows you to create, manage, and track transportation orders, including complex scenarios such as multi-leg and multi-stop shipments.

Transportation planning: With SAP TM, you can optimize your transportation planning process, including carrier selection, route determination, load planning, and capacity optimization.

Execution and monitoring: SAP TM provides real-time visibility into transportation processes, enabling you to monitor shipments, track their progress, and handle exceptions effectively.

Freight cost management: The solution helps you manage and calculate freight costs accurately, including contract management, freight rate calculation, and cost settlement.

Event management: SAP TM offers event management capabilities to track and manage transportation events such as delays, deviations, and milestones.

Integration with other systems: SAP TM seamlessly integrates with other SAP modules and external systems to ensure end-to-end visibility and process efficiency.

1.3 Benefits of Implementing SAP TM

Implementing SAP TM can bring significant advantages to your organization. Here are some key benefits:

Enhanced operational efficiency: SAP TM streamlines transportation processes, reduces manual effort, and increases process automation, leading to improved operational efficiency.

Cost savings: Through optimized planning, improved carrier selection, and accurate cost calculation, SAP TM helps organizations reduce transportation costs and achieve cost savings.

Improved customer service: SAP TM enables better visibility into transportation processes, allowing organizations to provide accurate delivery information to customers and enhance their overall experience.

Real-time monitoring and reporting: With SAP TM's monitoring and reporting capabilities, organizations can access real-time data and analytics to make informed decisions and proactively address issues.

Scalability and flexibility: SAP TM is a scalable solution that can accommodate growing business needs and adapt to changing market conditions.

Chapter 2: Getting Started with SAP TM

In this section, we'll guide you through the initial steps of getting started with SAP Transportation Management (TM). We'll cover the system requirements, installation and configuration process, as well as how to navigate the SAP TM user interface.

2.1 System Requirements and Prerequisites

Before installing SAP TM, it's important to ensure that your system meets the necessary requirements. Here are some key considerations:

Hardware requirements: Verify that your hardware meets the minimum specifications recommended by SAP for running SAP TM. This includes CPU, memory, and storage requirements.

Software requirements: Check the compatibility matrix provided by SAP to determine the compatible operating system, database, and other required software versions.

SAP NetWeaver platform: SAP TM is typically deployed on the SAP NetWeaver platform. Make sure you have the appropriate version of SAP NetWeaver installed.

Licenses and authorizations: Ensure that you have the necessary licenses and authorizations to install and use SAP TM. Contact your SAP representative for license procurement and activation.

2.2 Installation and Configuration of SAP TM

Now that you've verified the system requirements, let's proceed with the installation and configuration of SAP TM. Follow these steps:

Step 1: Obtain the SAP TM installation media or software package from SAP. This typically includes installation files and documentation.

Step 2: Read the installation guide provided by SAP for detailed instructions on the installation process. Pay attention to any specific prerequisites or additional software components that need to be installed.

Step 3: Execute the installation program and follow the on-screen instructions. Provide the necessary inputs, such as installation directory, database configuration, and system landscape details.

Step 4: After the installation is complete, perform the post-installation steps as outlined in the installation guide. These steps may include configuring communication channels, setting up transport routes, and activating necessary services.

Step 5: Apply any necessary support packages or patches to ensure your SAP TM system is up to date and compliant with the latest enhancements and bug fixes.

2.3 Navigating the SAP TM User Interface

Once your SAP TM system is installed and configured, it's time to familiarize yourself with the user interface. SAP TM offers a comprehensive and intuitive interface for managing transportation processes. Here are some key elements to be aware of:

Launchpad: The SAP TM launchpad serves as the central access point for all SAP TM functionalities. It provides easy navigation to various applications, dashboards, and reports.

Tiles and Apps: The launchpad consists of tiles that represent different applications or specific functions within SAP TM. Clicking on a tile opens the corresponding app or screen.

Navigation bar: The navigation bar allows you to switch between different areas of SAP TM, such as order management, planning, execution, and reporting. Use the navigation bar to access the desired module or function.

Search and Filters: SAP TM provides search and filter capabilities to help you locate specific data or transactions quickly. Utilize these features to find relevant information within the system.

Contextual menus: Contextual menus provide additional options and actions based on the selected object or transaction. Right-clicking on an item or using the context menu button reveals a list of available actions.

Personalization: SAP TM allows you to personalize your user interface by adjusting settings such as screen layouts, favorites, and default values. Customize the interface to suit your preferences and work style.

Congratulations! You have successfully completed the installation and configuration of SAP TM and gained familiarity with the user interface. In the next chapter, we'll delve into the essential master data management processes within SAP TM. Stay tuned!

Chapter 3: Master Data Management

In this section, we'll explore the critical aspect of master data management within SAP Transportation Management (TM). Master data forms the foundation for effective transportation planning, execution, and reporting. We'll cover key elements such as business partners, locations, transportation zones, lanes, and resources.

3.1 Managing Business Partners and Locations

Business partners and locations are essential entities within SAP TM. They represent the parties involved in transportation processes, such as customers, vendors, carriers, and warehouses. Here's how you can manage them:

Step 1: Create Business Partners: In SAP TM, navigate to the Business Partner application. Here, you can create and maintain business partner master data by providing relevant information such as name, address, contact details, and identification numbers.

Step 2: Define Locations: Locations are the physical places associated with business partners, such as ship-to locations, loading points, or warehouses. Access the Location

Management application and create location records, specifying details like address, coordinates, and capacity.

Step 3: Establish Relationships: Establish relationships between business partners and locations to enable seamless integration across processes. For example, link a customer business partner with their respective ship-to locations for accurate order management.

3.2 Configuring Transportation Zones and Lanes

Transportation zones and lanes play a crucial role in transportation planning and optimization. Let's see how you can configure them in SAP TM:

Step 1: Define Transportation Zones: Transportation zones are geographic areas that determine transportation rules and restrictions. Access the Transportation Zone application and create zones based on your organizational structure or specific criteria, such as countries, regions, or postal codes.

Step 2: Configure Transportation Lanes: Transportation lanes define the routes between specific locations within transportation zones. In the Lane Management application, create lanes by specifying origin and destination locations, modes of transport, distance, and transit times.

Step 3: Assign Transportation Zones and Lanes: Assign transportation zones and lanes to relevant business partners, carriers, or shipping points to ensure accurate planning and execution. This association enables SAP TM to consider the appropriate transportation rules and constraints for each transaction.

3.3 Defining Transportation Resources

Transportation resources, such as vehicles, carriers, and drivers, are vital for effective transportation management. Let's explore how to define and manage them:

Step 1: Set up Vehicles and Equipment: In SAP TM, navigate to the Vehicle Management application and create vehicle records, including details like registration numbers, dimensions, weight limits, and maintenance schedules. You can also manage equipment, such as containers or trailers, associated with vehicles.

Step 2: Configure Carriers: Carriers are transportation service providers. In the Carrier Management application, create carrier master data by specifying information such as company details, contact information, carrier capabilities, and equipment availability.

Step 3: Assign Drivers: If you manage driver information within SAP TM, assign drivers to vehicles or carriers. This linkage ensures accurate driver assignment during transportation planning and execution.

3.4 Creating Transportation Networks and Routes

Transportation networks and routes define the connections between locations and the sequence of stops for transportation activities. Here's how you can create them:

Step 1: Define Transportation Networks: In SAP TM's Network Management application, create transportation networks to represent your organizational structure or distribution network. Specify the nodes (locations) within the network and define relationships between them.

Step 2: Configure Routes: Routes define the sequence of stops within a transportation network. Utilize the Route Management application to create routes, assign locations to them, and set up routing rules, such as specific carriers or transportation modes.

Step 3: Optimize Networks and Routes: Optimize your transportation networks and routes using SAP TM's optimization capabilities. Consider factors like transportation costs, lead times, capacity constraints, and service levels to find the most efficient and cost-effective solutions.

Congratulations! You've learned the essentials of master data management within SAP TM. In the next chapter, we'll dive into the order management process, covering the creation, processing, and tracking of transportation orders. Stay tuned!

Chapter 4: Order Management

In this chapter, we'll explore the order management process within SAP Transportation Management (TM). Order management involves the creation, processing, and tracking of transportation orders, enabling you to efficiently manage your transportation operations.

4.1 Creating Transportation Orders

Transportation orders represent the transportation requirements of your organization. They can be created manually or automatically generated based on various factors such as sales orders, delivery requests, or production orders. Let's go through the process of creating transportation orders in SAP TM:

Step 1: Access the Transportation Order Management application in SAP TM.

Step 2: Click on the "Create Order" button to initiate the order creation process.

Step 3: Enter the relevant details for the transportation order, such as order type, order date, requested delivery date, and associated business partner or customer.

Step 4: Specify the transportation requirements, including the origin and destination locations, the mode of transport, preferred carrier, and any special handling instructions.

Step 5: Add the items or products to be transported, including their quantities, weights, dimensions, and any specific packaging requirements.

Step 6: Validate the order details and save the transportation order in the system.

4.2 Order-Based Planning

Once the transportation order is created, SAP TM offers order-based planning capabilities to optimize the transportation process and determine the most efficient way to fulfill the order. This includes carrier selection, route determination, and load planning. Here's how order-based planning works:

Step 1: Select the transportation order you want to plan in the Transportation Order Management application.

Step 2: Click on the "Plan Order" button to trigger the planning process.

Step 3: SAP TM will evaluate the transportation order details, including the transportation requirements, available carriers, transportation zones, and lane information.

Step 4: The system will determine the best carrier based on predefined criteria such as cost, service level, carrier capabilities, and any specific requirements.

Step 5: SAP TM will then determine the optimal route considering factors like distance, transit times, mode of transport, and any specific routing rules defined in the system.

Step 6: If the transportation order includes multiple items or products, SAP TM will perform load planning to consolidate items onto appropriate vehicles or containers, optimizing capacity utilization.

Step 7: Review and validate the planned results, including the selected carrier, route, and load assignment.

Step 8: Save the planning results, and the transportation order will be updated with the planned details.

4.3 Advanced Order Processing Options

SAP TM offers advanced order processing options to handle complex scenarios and optimize transportation operations. Here are some key functionalities:

Order Consolidation: If you have multiple transportation orders with similar characteristics, SAP TM allows you to consolidate them into a single shipment, reducing costs and improving efficiency.

Order Splitting: In cases where a transportation order cannot be fulfilled in a single shipment due to capacity or other constraints, SAP TM enables you to split the order into multiple shipments and plan them accordingly.

Backorder Processing: If a transportation order cannot be immediately fulfilled due to various reasons such as stock unavailability or capacity constraints, SAP TM provides backorder processing capabilities to track and manage these delayed orders.

Exception Handling: SAP TM includes features to manage and handle exceptions that may occur during the transportation process, such as delays, route deviations, or order cancellations. These exceptions can be tracked, monitored, and addressed effectively within the system.

4.4 Integration with SAP Sales and Distribution (SD) and Other Modules

SAP TM seamlessly integrates with other SAP modules, including Sales and Distribution (SD), to ensure end-to-end visibility and smooth information flow across the organization. The integration between SAP TM and SAP SD enables the automatic creation of transportation orders based on sales orders or delivery requests. It also allows for the synchronization of data, such as customer information, delivery dates, and order quantities, between the two modules.

Additionally, SAP TM integrates with other relevant modules such as Materials Management (MM) for procurement processes, Production Planning (PP) for transportation requirements related to production orders, and Warehouse Management (WM) for managing transportation-related activities within the warehouse.

The integration between SAP TM and these modules ensures a holistic approach to transportation management, enabling accurate planning, execution, and tracking of transportation orders within the broader supply chain processes.

Congratulations! You have learned the essentials of order management within SAP TM. In the next chapter, we'll delve into transportation planning, including route determination, carrier selection, and load optimization. Stay tuned!

Chapter 5: Transportation Planning

In this chapter, we'll dive into the transportation planning process within SAP Transportation Management (TM). Effective transportation planning is crucial for optimizing routes, selecting the right carriers, and achieving efficient load utilization. We'll cover key aspects such as route determination, carrier selection, load planning, and optimization techniques.

5.1 Route Determination

Route determination involves finding the most suitable route for transporting goods from the origin location to the destination location. SAP TM provides flexible route determination capabilities based on predefined rules and parameters. Here's how you can determine routes in SAP TM:

Step 1: Access the Transportation Order Management application in SAP TM.

Step 2: Select the relevant transportation order for which you want to determine the route.

Step 3: Click on the "Determine Route" button to initiate the route determination process.

Step 4: SAP TM will evaluate factors such as transportation zones, transportation lanes, carrier preferences, transit times, and any specific routing rules defined in the system.

Step 5: Based on these factors, the system will determine the optimal route considering distance, cost, service level, and other criteria.

Step 6: Review and validate the determined route. You can also make manual adjustments if necessary.

Step 7: Save the determined route in the transportation order.

5.2 Carrier Selection

Selecting the right carrier is crucial for ensuring timely and cost-effective transportation. SAP TM provides carrier selection capabilities based on various criteria such as cost, service level, carrier capabilities, and specific requirements. Here's how you can select carriers in SAP TM:

Step 1: Access the Transportation Order Management application in SAP TM.

Step 2: Select the relevant transportation order for which you want to select a carrier.

Step 3: Click on the "Select Carrier" button to initiate the carrier selection process.

Step 4: SAP TM will consider factors such as transportation zones, transportation lanes, carrier preferences, pricing agreements, and carrier capabilities.

Step 5: Based on these factors, the system will suggest the most suitable carrier for the transportation order.

Step 6: Review the carrier suggestions, compare their capabilities, costs, and service levels.

Step 7: Select the preferred carrier and save the carrier selection in the transportation order.

5.3 Load Planning and Optimization Techniques

Efficient load planning and optimization help maximize the utilization of available transportation resources, such as vehicles or containers, reducing costs and improving efficiency. SAP TM offers advanced load planning and optimization techniques. Let's explore them:

Step 1: Access the Transportation Order Management application in SAP TM.

Step 2: Select the relevant transportation order for which you want to perform load planning and optimization.

Step 3: Click on the "Plan Load" button to initiate the load planning process.

Step 4: SAP TM will consider factors such as order quantities, product dimensions, weight limits, vehicle capacities, and any specific loading constraints defined in the system.

Step 5: Based on these factors, the system will optimize the load assignment, consolidating multiple items or products onto appropriate vehicles or containers.

Step 6: Review the load planning results, including the assigned items, their quantities, and the allocated transportation resources.

Step 7: Make manual adjustments if necessary and save the load planning results in the transportation order.

SAP TM also offers advanced optimization techniques such as multi-stop optimization, which finds the most efficient sequence of stops for multiple transportation orders, minimizing overall transportation distances and costs.

Congratulations! You've learned the essentials of transportation planning within SAP TM. In the next chapter, we'll explore execution and monitoring, including tendering, tracking, and real-time visibility of shipments. Stay tuned!

Chapter 6: Execution and Monitoring

In this chapter, we'll explore the execution and monitoring process within SAP Transportation Management (TM). Execution involves tendering transportation orders to carriers, tracking and tracing shipments, and handling exceptions. Monitoring provides real-time visibility into transportation processes and enables effective decision-making. Let's dive in!

6.1 Tendering and Carrier Collaboration

Tendering is the process of assigning transportation orders to carriers for execution. SAP TM provides functionalities to facilitate tendering and carrier collaboration. Here's how you can tender transportation orders in SAP TM:

Step 1: Access the Transportation Order Management application in SAP TM.

Step 2: Select the relevant transportation order for which you want to tender to a carrier.

Step 3: Click on the "Tender" button to initiate the tendering process.

Step 4: SAP TM will generate a tender document containing all relevant order details, including pickup and delivery locations, scheduled dates, and any specific instructions.

Step 5: Send the tender document to the selected carrier through the configured communication channels, such as email or electronic data interchange (EDI).

Step 6: Track the status of the tendered order, including carrier acceptance or rejection.

Step 7: Once the carrier accepts the tender, update the transportation order with the carrier information and confirmation.

SAP TM also enables carrier collaboration by providing carriers with access to a carrier portal. This portal allows carriers to view, confirm, and update tendered orders, ensuring smooth communication and collaboration between the shipper and carriers.

6.2 Tracking and Tracing Shipments

Tracking and tracing shipments in real-time is crucial for maintaining visibility and proactively addressing any potential issues. SAP TM provides tracking and tracing capabilities to monitor shipments throughout the transportation process. Here's how you can track and trace shipments in SAP TM:

Step 1: Access the Shipment Management application in SAP TM.

Step 2: Search for the relevant shipment using criteria such as shipment number, transportation order, or carrier.

Step 3: View the current status of the shipment, including pickup and delivery events, milestones, and any exceptions or delays.

Step 4: Track the physical location of the shipment using technologies such as GPS tracking or RFID tags, if available.

Step 5: Utilize SAP TM's event management functionalities to capture and monitor transportation events, such as delays, deviations, or goods receipts.

Step 6: Communicate with carriers, warehouses, or other stakeholders to obtain real-time updates and resolve any issues.

Step 7: Generate reports and analytics to analyze shipment performance, on-time delivery rates, and other key performance indicators (KPIs).

6.3 Handling Delays and Exceptions

Delays and exceptions can occur during transportation due to various factors such as traffic congestion, weather conditions, or unexpected events. SAP TM provides functionalities to handle and manage these delays and exceptions effectively. Here's how you can handle delays and exceptions in SAP TM:

Step 1: Monitor the shipment's status and events using the tracking and tracing capabilities in SAP TM.

Step 2: Identify any delays or exceptions reported through event management functionalities or communication with carriers.

Step 3: Assess the impact of the delay or exception on the transportation process, customer commitments, and overall supply chain.

Step 4: Take necessary actions to mitigate the delay or exception, such as re-routing, rescheduling, or arranging alternative transportation options.

Step 5: Communicate and collaborate with carriers, customers, and other stakeholders to keep them informed about the situation and any necessary adjustments.

Step 6: Update the shipment status and event information in SAP TM to reflect the resolution of the delay or exception.

SAP TM's exception management capabilities allow you to set up rules and workflows to automate the handling of specific exceptions, triggering notifications and escalations as needed.

6.4 Real-time Monitoring and Reporting

Real-time monitoring and reporting provide valuable insights into transportation processes, enabling data-driven decision-making and performance analysis. SAP TM offers monitoring and reporting functionalities to track key metrics and generate reports. Here's how you can monitor and report on transportation processes in SAP TM:

Step 1: Utilize SAP TM's dashboard and monitoring tools to access real-time information on transportation processes, such as order statuses, shipment statuses, and key performance indicators (KPIs).

Step 2: Configure personalized dashboards to display relevant metrics and trends based on your specific requirements and roles.

Step 3: Generate standard or customized reports to analyze transportation performance, carrier performance, cost analysis, and other relevant metrics.

Step 4: Utilize SAP TM's analytics tools to perform in-depth analysis, visualize data, and identify areas for improvement.

Step 5: Share reports and insights with stakeholders, such as management, customers, or carriers, to drive collaboration and continuous improvement.

By effectively leveraging real-time monitoring and reporting capabilities in SAP TM, you can gain visibility into transportation processes, identify bottlenecks, and make informed decisions to optimize your transportation operations.

Congratulations! You've learned about the execution and monitoring process within SAP TM. In the next chapter, we'll delve into freight cost management, including freight cost calculation, rate agreements, and cost reporting. Stay tuned!

Chapter 7: Freight Cost Management

In this chapter, we'll explore freight cost management within SAP Transportation Management (TM). Freight cost management involves accurately calculating, managing, and analyzing transportation costs. We'll cover key aspects such as freight cost calculation, configuring freight agreements and rates, cost settlement, and cost reporting and analysis.

7.1 Setting up Freight Cost Calculation

Accurate freight cost calculation is essential for evaluating the financial impact of transportation activities. SAP TM provides functionalities to calculate freight costs based on various factors such as distance, weight, volume, carrier rates, and any additional charges. Here's how you can set up freight cost calculation in SAP TM:

Step 1: Access the Freight Order Management application in SAP TM.

Step 2: Define the necessary cost calculation parameters, such as cost elements, cost types, and rate types, based on your organization's requirements.

Step 3: Configure the cost calculation formulas to define how the various cost elements are calculated. This may include factors like distance-based rates, weight-based rates, fuel surcharges, or accessorial charges.

Step 4: Set up condition types to represent the different cost components, such as freight charges, surcharges, taxes, or discounts.

Step 5: Define the calculation rules for each condition type, considering the relevant factors, rate tables, and pricing agreements.

Step 6: Validate the freight cost calculation by testing it with sample transportation orders and comparing the calculated costs with expected values.

7.2 Configuring Freight Agreements and Rates

Freight agreements and rates play a crucial role in determining transportation costs. SAP TM allows you to configure and manage freight agreements and rates with carriers or service providers. Here's how you can configure freight agreements and rates in SAP TM:

Step 1: Access the Freight Agreement Management application in SAP TM.

Step 2: Define the necessary freight agreement types based on your organization's requirements. Examples include spot agreements, volume-based agreements, or long-term contracts.

Step 3: Create freight agreements with carriers, specifying details such as effective dates, routes, transportation zones, service levels, and associated rates.

Step 4: Configure the rate tables within each freight agreement, defining the applicable rates based on factors like distance, weight, volume, transportation modes, or other relevant criteria.

Step 5: Maintain the rate records within each rate table, specifying the rates for different conditions, such as origin-destination pairs, weight ranges, or specific products.

Step 6: Validate the configured freight agreements and rates by testing them with sample transportation orders and comparing the calculated costs with the expected values.

7.3 Calculating and Settling Freight Costs

Once the freight cost calculation is set up and freight agreements are in place, SAP TM enables the calculation and settlement of freight costs. Here's how you can calculate and settle freight costs in SAP TM:

Step 1: Access the Freight Settlement application in SAP TM.

Step 2: Select the relevant freight orders or shipments for which you want to calculate and settle the freight costs.

Step 3: Trigger the freight cost calculation process, which takes into account the configured freight agreements, rates, and cost calculation formulas.

Step 4: SAP TM calculates the freight costs based on the applicable rates, conditions, and relevant factors of the transportation orders.

Step 5: Review and validate the calculated freight costs, ensuring they align with the agreed-upon rates and expected values.

Step 6: Settle the freight costs by creating settlement documents and generating accounting entries, which can be integrated with the financial accounting system for further processing.

7.4 Cost Reporting and Analysis

Cost reporting and analysis provide valuable insights into transportation expenses, allowing for better decision-making and cost optimization. SAP TM offers reporting and analysis functionalities to generate cost reports and perform in-depth analysis. Here's how you can perform cost reporting and analysis in SAP TM:

Step 1: Utilize SAP TM's reporting tools to access standard reports or create customized reports based on your specific cost analysis requirements.

Step 2: Generate reports to analyze freight costs by various dimensions, such as carrier, transportation mode, route, customer, or product.

Step 3: Utilize SAP TM's analytics capabilities to visualize cost data, identify cost trends, and compare actual costs against budgeted or planned costs.

Step 4: Perform cost analysis to identify areas for cost optimization, such as renegotiating freight agreements, optimizing transportation routes, or improving carrier selection.

Step 5: Share cost reports and insights with stakeholders, such as management, finance teams, or procurement, to drive cost-conscious decision-making and continuous improvement.

By effectively managing freight costs, calculating accurate costs, settling expenses, and analyzing cost data, you can optimize your transportation operations and drive cost savings within your supply chain.

Congratulations! You've learned about freight cost management within SAP TM. In the next chapter, we'll explore event management and analytics capabilities, enabling you to track and manage transportation events and leverage data-driven insights. Stay tuned!

Chapter 8: Event Management and Analytics

In this chapter, we'll delve into event management and analytics within SAP Transportation Management (TM). Event management enables you to track and manage transportation events, while analytics provides valuable insights for data-driven decision-making. Let's explore these capabilities in SAP TM.

8.1 Configuring Event Management

Event management allows you to track and manage transportation events, such as delays, deviations, or milestones, in real-time. SAP TM provides functionalities to configure event management based on your organization's requirements. Here's how you can configure event management in SAP TM:

Step 1: Access the Event Management application in SAP TM.

Step 2: Define the types of events you want to track, such as pickup, delivery, arrival at a milestone, departure from a location, or customs clearance.

Step 3: Configure event profiles to specify the relevant events for different types of transportation orders or shipments.

Step 4: Define the rules for event creation, including the conditions that trigger events, the associated transportation objects, and the recipients of event notifications.

Step 5: Configure event escalation and notification workflows to ensure timely communication and resolution of transportation events.

Step 6: Test the event management configuration by simulating transportation events and verifying the expected event creation and notification processes.

8.2 Creating and Managing Transportation Events

Once event management is configured, you can create and manage transportation events within SAP TM. Here's how you can create and manage transportation events:

Step 1: Access the Event Management application in SAP TM.

Step 2: Create transportation events manually or automatically based on predefined event creation rules.

Step 3: Specify the event type, event time, associated transportation object (such as transportation order or shipment), and any additional event-specific information.

Step 4: Assign events to relevant transportation orders or shipments to ensure accurate tracking and visibility.

Step 5: Monitor and manage transportation events in real-time, track their progress, and take necessary actions to address any deviations or exceptions.

Step 6: Communicate event updates to stakeholders such as carriers, customers, or internal teams through notifications or integration with communication channels.

8.3 Utilizing SAP TM Analytics and Reporting Tools

SAP TM provides powerful analytics and reporting tools to leverage transportation data and gain valuable insights. Here's how you can utilize analytics and reporting tools in SAP TM:

Step 1: Access the Analytics and Reporting applications in SAP TM.

Step 2: Utilize standard reports provided by SAP TM to analyze transportation performance, carrier performance, on-time delivery rates, and other key performance indicators (KPIs).

Step 3: Customize reports by selecting relevant dimensions, measures, and filters based on your specific reporting requirements.

Step 4: Leverage SAP TM's analytics capabilities to visualize transportation data using charts, graphs, or dashboards.

Step 5: Perform ad-hoc analysis by drilling down into transportation data, identifying patterns, and exploring relationships between different variables.

Step 6: Export reports or share them with stakeholders to facilitate data-driven decision-making, continuous improvement, and collaboration.

By effectively utilizing event management and analytics capabilities in SAP TM, you can track and manage transportation events in real-time, gain insights from transportation data, and make informed decisions to optimize your transportation processes.

Congratulations! You've learned about event management and analytics in SAP TM. In the next chapter, we'll explore integration with other SAP modules, enabling seamless information flow across different functionalities. Stay tuned!

Chapter 9: Integration with Other SAP Modules

In this chapter, we'll explore the integration capabilities of SAP Transportation Management (TM) with other SAP modules. Integration enables seamless information flow and synchronization between different functionalities within the SAP ecosystem. We'll focus on integration with SAP ERP, SAP Extended Warehouse Management (EWM), SAP Global Trade Services (GTS), and SAP Business Intelligence (BI).

9.1 Integration with SAP ERP

Integration between SAP TM and SAP ERP ensures smooth coordination between transportation management and other business processes such as procurement, sales, and materials management. Here's how SAP TM integrates with SAP ERP:

Step 1: Material Master Integration: SAP TM integrates with SAP ERP's Material Management (MM) module, allowing access to material master data, such as product descriptions, dimensions, weight, and packaging information. This data is essential for transportation planning and execution.

Step 2: Sales Integration: Integration with SAP Sales and Distribution (SD) module enables the automatic creation of transportation orders based on sales orders or delivery requests. Transportation requirements, such as delivery dates, quantities, and customer information, flow seamlessly from SD to TM.

Step 3: Procurement Integration: Integration with SAP ERP's procurement processes ensures the availability of transportation requirements related to purchase orders and inbound deliveries. This integration enables transportation planning based on procurement activities and provides visibility into the inbound transportation process.

Step 4: Financial Integration: SAP TM integrates with SAP ERP's Financial Accounting (FI) module to facilitate seamless cost settlement, generate accounting entries, and align transportation costs with financial processes.

9.2 Integration with SAP Extended Warehouse Management (EWM)

Integration between SAP TM and SAP Extended Warehouse Management (EWM) enables end-to-end visibility and control over transportation and warehouse operations. Here's how SAP TM integrates with SAP EWM:

Step 1: Outbound Integration: SAP TM communicates with SAP EWM to provide transportation details and instructions for outbound deliveries. This integration ensures that transportation orders and requirements are seamlessly transferred to the warehouse for loading and shipment preparation.

Step 2: Inbound Integration: SAP TM receives transportation requirements from SAP EWM for inbound deliveries, allowing for transportation planning and execution based on warehouse activities. This integration ensures that transportation arrangements are aligned with the receipt of goods into the warehouse.

Step 3: Event Synchronization: Transportation events, such as goods issue or goods receipt, are synchronized between SAP TM and SAP EWM, providing real-time visibility into the progress of transportation and warehouse operations.

9.3 Integration with SAP Global Trade Services (GTS)

Integration between SAP TM and SAP Global Trade Services (GTS) enables comprehensive management of international transportation and trade compliance. Here's how SAP TM integrates with SAP GTS:

Step 1: Compliance Checks: SAP TM integrates with SAP GTS to perform compliance checks during transportation planning and execution. This integration ensures adherence to legal and regulatory requirements related to customs, trade embargoes, and other trade compliance regulations.

Step 2: Trade Documentation: Integration with SAP GTS enables the generation of trade documentation, such as export declarations or import documentation, based on transportation data and compliance requirements. This integration ensures accurate and efficient handling of trade-related documentation.

Step 3: Customs Processes: SAP TM integrates with SAP GTS to exchange data with customs authorities, automate customs declarations, and streamline customs clearance processes. This integration facilitates efficient customs handling and reduces the risk of compliance errors.

9.4 Integration with SAP Business Intelligence (BI)

Integration between SAP TM and SAP Business Intelligence (BI) provides enhanced reporting and analytics capabilities for transportation data. Here's how SAP TM integrates with SAP BI:

Step 1: Data Extraction: SAP TM integrates with SAP BI to extract relevant transportation data for reporting and analysis purposes. This integration ensures the availability of up-to-date and accurate data for decision-making.

Step 2: Data Transformation and Modeling: SAP BI performs data transformation, modeling, and aggregation to create meaningful transportation reports and analytical views. This integration allows for the consolidation and visualization of transportation data from various sources.

Step 3: Reporting and Dashboards: SAP BI provides comprehensive reporting and dashboarding functionalities to analyze transportation KPIs, track performance, and monitor key trends. This integration enables data-driven decision-making and continuous improvement in transportation management.

By integrating SAP TM with other SAP modules such as ERP, EWM, GTS, and BI, you can achieve end-to-end visibility, streamline processes, and leverage the full potential of your SAP ecosystem.

Congratulations! You've learned about the integration capabilities of SAP TM with other SAP modules. In the next chapter, we'll discuss best practices for successful implementation and ongoing management of SAP TM. Stay tuned!

Chapter 10: Best Practices for SAP TM Implementation and Management

In this final chapter, we'll discuss best practices for the successful implementation and ongoing management of SAP Transportation Management (TM). These practices will help you maximize the benefits of SAP TM and ensure efficient and effective transportation management within your organization.

10.1 Define Clear Objectives and Scope

Before implementing SAP TM, clearly define your objectives and scope. Understand the specific challenges you aim to address, such as improving transportation efficiency, reducing costs, or enhancing customer service. Define the scope of the implementation, including the modules and functionalities you will utilize. This clarity will guide the implementation process and ensure alignment with your organization's goals.

10.2 Engage Stakeholders and Establish a Project Team

Involve key stakeholders from different departments, such as transportation, logistics, IT, finance, and customer service, in the implementation process. Establish a dedicated project team comprising individuals with relevant expertise and representation from various functions. This collaborative approach will ensure that the implementation considers the needs and perspectives of all stakeholders.

10.3 Conduct Comprehensive Business Process Analysis

Perform a thorough analysis of your existing transportation processes and identify areas for improvement. Map out your current processes, identify pain points, and define the desired future-state processes. This analysis will help you align SAP TM with your business requirements and optimize the configuration and customization of the system.

10.4 Ensure Adequate Data Quality and Migration

Data plays a critical role in SAP TM. Ensure that your data is accurate, complete, and properly structured. Cleanse and validate your data before migrating it to SAP TM to avoid issues during implementation. Develop a robust data migration strategy, including data extraction, transformation, and loading processes. Verify the migrated data to ensure its integrity and accuracy within SAP TM.

10.5 Customize and Configure Appropriately

Tailor SAP TM to meet your specific business needs through appropriate customization and configuration. Leverage the standard functionalities and adapt them to align with your processes and requirements. Avoid excessive customization that may hinder future upgrades or cause maintenance challenges. Strike a balance between customization and utilizing standard SAP TM capabilities.

10.6 Invest in User Training and Change Management

Provide comprehensive training to end-users on how to effectively utilize SAP TM. Offer both system training and process training to ensure users understand the system functionalities as well as the optimized processes. Implement change management practices to facilitate smooth adoption of SAP TM within your organization. Communicate the benefits, address concerns, and provide ongoing support to users during and after the implementation.

10.7 Establish Key Performance Indicators (KPIs) and Metrics

Define key performance indicators (KPIs) and metrics to measure the success of your SAP TM implementation. Identify the relevant KPIs based on your business objectives, such as on-time delivery rate, transportation cost per unit, or carrier performance. Continuously monitor and analyze these metrics to identify areas for improvement and drive continuous optimization.

10.8 Embrace Continuous Improvement and System Enhancements

SAP TM is a dynamic solution that evolves with your business needs and industry changes. Stay informed about the latest updates, enhancements, and best practices in SAP TM. Regularly evaluate your transportation processes, identify opportunities for improvement, and leverage system enhancements to optimize your transportation management.

By following these best practices, you can ensure a successful implementation and effective management of SAP Transportation Management (TM) within your organization.

Congratulations! You've completed the tutorial book on SAP TM. We hope this resource has provided you with valuable insights and guidance on learning and utilizing SAP TM to optimize your transportation management processes. Good luck with your SAP TM journey!

www.ingramcontent.com/pod-product-compliance
Lightning Source LLC
LaVergne TN
LVHW051620050326
832903LV00033B/4585